MW00423302

POETRY THAT ENTERS THE MIND AND WARMS THE HEART

The Wisdom of God creates poets.

James T. O'Connor
The Hidden Manna

Poetry That Enters the Mind and Warms the Heart

Cover image from a painting by Pam Cole

Book design
with images composed or chosen
by James Kent Ridley

ISBN-13: 978-1511626620
ISBN-10: 1511626623

Ad Majorem Dei Gloriam

Published by Goodbooks Media

GOODBOOKS MEDIA

3453 Aransas
Corpus Christi, Texas, 78411
goodbooksmedia.com

ACKNOWLEDGEMENT

I am pleased to express my gratitude to Ronda Chervin for leading me to Goodbooks, to James Ridley for his cultivated taste in poetry, and to all the members of my family for their inspiration.

DEDICATION

This book is dedicated to Dae, a person of prayer, and a
painter of words and images.

TABLE OF CONTENTS

INTRODUCTION

obert Frost came close to the meaning of our title, *Poetry That Enters the Mind and Warms the Heart*, when he said that "Poetry is when an emotion has found its thought and the thought has found words." The interplay between emotion, thought, and verbal expression is essential to poetry. This book of poetry is perhaps a little unusual insofar as it articulates the thought and emotion before they have passed into poetic expression.

Poetry can be intimidating because of its economy of words, its metaphorical language, and its frequent allusions to literature. The explanatory lead-ins prior to each poem are intended to supply a context so that each poem is more easily grasped and appreciated. I would like to think that the following poems evoke in the reader something close to a remembrance of his or her own personal feelings and experiences. Poetic expression has great value, and, sadly, it is severely undervalued in today's highly mobile and materialistic society. I agree, therefore, with Matthew Arnold's statement that, "Poetry is simply the most beautiful, impressive, and widely effective mode of saying things, and hence its importance."

"The poet," writes poet and scholar, John Crowe Ransom, "perpetuates in his poem an order of existence which in actual life is constantly crumbling beneath his touch." Lived experiences are often too rich and deep to be adequately retained by the memory. Poetry endeavors to bring back to life some of the magic and charm of past experiences. Poetry, therefore, is a beautiful way of remembering what it would impoverish us to forget.

It is sincerely hoped that the reader will find not only enjoyment from the following poems, but a better appreciation for the value of poetry and the important place it holds both in society and in one's life.

Donald DeMarco
October 20, 2014
Kitchener, Ontario

POETRY THAT ENTERS THE MIND
AND WARMS THE HEART

LIGHT VERSUS DARK
VERSES

Light Verse

ow does one express thanks to his ophthalmologist after he performed two successful cataract surgeries?

A mere "thank you" seems woefully inadequate.

With a nod to Dante's *terza rima* and his regard for the splendor of light, I wrote him a poem which he found "awesome" and suitable for framing.

It is most reassuring to be able to see eye-to-eye as well as speak heart-to-heart with one's eye doctor.

Don Marquis may have been hasty when he said that writing poetry is like dropping rose petals into the Grand Canyon and waiting for the echo.

My improved vision gives me a better appreciation of St. Bonaventure's claim that among all things in the universe, that which most clearly resembles God is light (*"Lux inter omnia corporalia maxime assimilatur luci aeterni"*).

God said, "Let there be light".
Attempting to challenge His Right,
Time said, "Let there be night";

Yet God's work had only begun,
Not wanting the light from the sun
To be dimmed in the eye or undone,

Granted science and skill to a few
Who learned what they needed to do
To return Heaven and Earth into view,

While lifting the curtain of night--
An action that sets things aright--
Restoring the splendor of sight.

Transubstantiation

n April 24, 2007, Americo DeMarco was interred at Notre Dame cemetery in Fall River, MA. His great-granddaughter, Marion, who is named after Marion DeMarco, the deceased's wife of 70 years, stepped out of line to pick dandelions. She then presented the flowers to her 102-year-old namesake, who, without her eyeglasses, mistook the dandelions for something nobler.

I thought that this tender and meaningful moment should be captured in a poem, the way a picture is captured by a camera. The following poem has several levels of meaning, not the least of which is resurrection.

To a three-year old,
a cemetery is not a grave-site
but an Elysian field
where flowers bloom
for gathering and presenting,
one by one,
to antiquated folks who wrongly view
dandelions as weeds
and
plucking them on solemn occasions
as violating sacred protocol.

And yet, if one is old enough,
she can journey back to joyful childhood
and join her youthful benefactor
on a plane more real
than where most people dwell.

Thus, wheelchaired and unbespectacled,
great in years and ultra-grand in motherhood,
she fittingly mistook her present
for something far more precious.

Love transubstantiated our gifts,
both in giving and receiving;

The heart sees deeper and more truly
than what our rules allow.

Sacrifice

eaching is not easy if you want to reach the student's heart. I recall one former student of mine who, on the one hand, invited me to reach her heart, while on the other hand, remained very protective. In this case, one must empty himself of all self-interest so that the student does not fear being imposed upon or in some way being manipulated. For psychiatrist Viktor E. Frankl, "What is to shed light must endure burning." I felt that I was carrying out this process until there was a successful transmission of light. Teaching, particularly on a moral level, requires sacrifice. Christ came into the world to bring Light. At the same time, he was the Sacrificial Lamb.

This particular poem is richly analogical and can be read on 10 different levels, from the physical suggestion of a candle, to Christ's Resurrection.

This slender stem -
the wax-imprisoned
soul
of candle's being -
Ignited,
starts the
slow
descent
toward death;
Converting its encasing
flesh
to molten drops
than hang
like tears upon a cheek,
the painful price
of
making life
more
luminous,
Until -
substance spent,
cylindrical shell
dissolved -
it makes its final peace
with night,
consumed
by its own passion
to shed
light.

DREAMS

uring the era of Stalin's "Planned Starvation" in the Ukraine, a stout-hearted grandfather would tell members of his family to get up and "rouse the lion in your soul". When I came across this note of encouragement in an article, I was moved by the grandfather's courage, care, and hope. It was, in fact, the inspiration for "Dreams". Two of his descendents, Michael and Harry Medved, after coming to America, have done very well for themselves in the entertainment field. It so happened that I was invited to speak at a Pan-American conference on the family where Michael Medved would be the principal speaker. I brought along my poem hoping that I would have the chance to give it to him. He was not easy to find. I had resigned myself to going to bed when three friends called out to me and wanted to tell me about "rousing the lion in the soul". It was an astonishing coincidence made even more astonishing when my friend Zoe said to me, "Look over your shoulder". I then found myself looking directly into the eyes of none other than Michael Medved. I gave him a copy of the poem and he signed my copy of his book, *The Golden Turkey Awards*: "For Dr. DeMarco – Fine scholar – Fine Poet – and – kindred spirit".

May all your dreams be plausible
And every plan realistic,
Dismiss all thoughts of heroism
And ideals atavistic:
Of hope to change the hearts of men
To make them brave and bold
Or rouse the lion in you soul -
You'll die before you're old.

For time is swift and life is short,
No need to spoil the fun,
Take comfort in the second best,
Look out for number one,
Insist on what is guaranteed,
Security must come first,
Grab all the gusto you can get,
To slake your ravaged thirst.

And when the reaper comes along
To draw the final curtain,
In solemn tones he will proclaim
The one thing that is certain:
That since you dreamed of nothing more
Than solid plausibility,
Although your dreams, in fact, came true,
They cursed you with sterility.

NEW YEAR'S EVE

ur small circle of friends has convened for the past several years on the last day of the year to say goodbye to the past year and welcome the next. It is a festive occasion sprinkled with food, fun, and fellowship. A forward thinking member of the circle proposed that each member write and recite a poem for our next celebration. My wife forgot to pass this information along to me and, although I did write "New Year's Eve," it was written too late and unavailable for recitation. Upon reading the poem, my wife tried to console me by stating that no one would understand it anyway.

The poem passes from the ritual of welcoming the New Year to a more serious expression of hope that attaches itself not to one more year in the secular world, but to the life of each individual as a whole.

We all remember how, amidst a flurry of
Handshakes and a chorus of encouraging words,
We believed that the New Year's Child,
Innocent as daybreak, fresh as the morning dew,
Brought hope and a broad horizon
To an old and weary world;

But the world is never kind to innocence and youth;
Within that span of a dozen months
The world shattered that hope and
Erased that bright horizon,
Reducing our youth-filled harbinger to
A spent and sullen satire of itself.

We survey the carnage of yesteryear
And wonder why we ever hoped at all;
Yet not to hope is not to live,
Build up strength that lets us
Abide the small defeats and momentary setbacks,
Convey to others that there is more
To who we are at the present time
And another place where hope plays out its final
act.
As it steps aside to introduce
What it promised from the start – our everlasting
joy.

What the Leaves Are Saying

s it possible for nature to tell us something? In Shakespeare's As You Like It, he speaks of finding "tongues in trees, books in running brooks", and "sermons in stone". How is this possible? The answer lies in the use of metaphor. Aristotle held that the "metaphor most brings about learning". He gives the example of Homer using the word "stubble" to refer to old age since both old age and stubble belong to the genus of things that have lost their bloom. In other words, "stubble" tells us something about ourselves and therefore advances our learning.

The falling leaves resemble, metaphorically, advancing age, just as the arching limbs remind us of hands held high in prayer. Also, the brevity of the seasons suggests the shortness of life. But the poem transcends mere nature, implying that we human beings, though mortal, await our re-birth in a new life.

Pale, desiccated leaves, fluttering in the autumn
wind,
Imperiled by the same breath that gives them
Their metaphoric meaning;
Clinging heroically and desperately to withering
stems,
Not knowing what advancing moment
Will detach them from their vital source
And send them plummeting to their grave;
Anxiously trying to tell, in whispering agitations, a
world
That can no longer read what they are trying to say:
Life is short;
Time is precious;
The verdant hope that sprang in May
Is now fulfilled, yet not in
Ecstasy but desolation;
Windswept trees will solemnly stand
With leave-less, outstretched arms,
Configuring an arching prayer and
The hope of Regeneration.

ON CLOSING

he comparison between a customer's affection for his favorite grocery store and the love between Romeo and Juliet is hyperbole, or an exaggeration. It crosses into the realm of the comical. The play on sweetness continues throughout the poem, including its application to such amenities as coffee and flowers.

The word "Supermarket" seems to apply to every large grocery store. However, its meaning is blunted by reiteration. If everything is "great," then "great" loses its greatness. But when we emancipate "super" from its absorption into "market," it regains its meaning. Thus, we can say that not every Supermarket is a super market.

I pinned my anonymous poem to the store's bulletin board and enjoyed the smiles and chuckles it evoked from passers-by.

Parting is such sweet sorrow,
As Shakespeare once explained,
But no such sweetness marks a closing,
The two are not the same;

We who are your customers
Share your sweetless sorrow;
May more careful management
Secure a bright tomorrow;

We'll miss your pleasant atmosphere,
The spacious aisles and bright displays,
The morning coffee you provided
Made sweeter by your courteous ways;

The sales and specials and the "freshness",
The books, the flowers, the extra things,
The generous hours that you were open,
The royal touch that made us feel like kings;

We stand in gratitude and salute you,
May your future be more kind;
For us the bitter truth is this:
A more super market will be hard to find.

In A Word

agree with Percy Bysshe Shelley, though not often. But I like his description of the poet as, "a nightingale who sits in darkness and sings to cheer its own solitude with sweet sounds". There are times when a poet can have no loftier an ambition than to write a poem that contains nothing more than "sweet sounds". "In a Word" contains a dozen words that surrender themselves with the same sweet syllable. It is like a dozen roses presented to a fair maiden.

St. Robert Southwell, 16th century Jesuit priest and poet, remarked that, "What thought can think, another thought can mend." The same can be said for words. Words can either hurt or heal. The sweet sounds of soothing words can go a long way in bringing cheer to anyone who sits in darkness.

Super St. Catherine of Siena
has words with Pope Gregory XI

In a word
You are
Vivacious
Though some might say
Loquacious
Or possibly
Flirtatious
But never
Contumacious
For that would not be
Gracious
But terribly
Mendacious
For your charm is quite
Contagious
A model for the
Voracious;
Yet if I could be
Audacious
With license broad and
Spacious
And you any more
Precocious
You'd be...
SUPERCALIFRAGILISTICEXPIALIDOCIUS.

Divided Loyalty

any of us have created an alter-ego, that other self that we would prefer to be. Life can be a tension between our true selves, though often dormant, and that image of ourselves that intoxicates us. We all have a destiny, though it may not emerge and become clear until later in life. But it is never easy to follow one's destiny for it requires sacrifice, hard work, and meeting formidable challenges. The Christian must pick up and carry his cross on a daily basis. Personal authenticity comes at a price and is not easily achieved. Life's difficulties are sent to purify us.

My friend, who was intrigued by Tinker Bell, became a nurse, wife, and mother. She discarded the pixie dust and became the person she was destined to be from birth.

When Jupiter and Venus,
Mercury and Saturn,
Were in agreeable alignment,
And a little girl was lost in sweet surrender to the
ministry of sleep,
Two spirits entered her quiet world, embodied in
a dream,
Offering gifts, promising
blessings,
But more than her innocent heart could
comprehend:

The first,
a light-winged fairy, told of magic
powers,
Charms that would make the universe obey
Her every wish without delay,
An easy life,
Devoid of strife,
Pixie dust that turns all toil to
play;
"My name," she said, "is Tinker
Bell,"
And then she flew away.

The second,
an angel with a heart-shaped face, outlined a more
demanding course,
Not of magic spells that always grant your
way,
But tired feet that run to help, and trembling hands
that pray,
Smiles for the meek,
Arms for the weak,
All instruments to test your love and place it on
display;
"My name," she said, "is Pamela,
And I am here to stay."

EVE'S ARRIVAL

den was Paradise. But, before Eve's arrival, something essential was missing. Adam, no doubt, was not satisfied as a gardener and zookeeper. What was missing was a vibrant love between two human beings.

We can imagine how well received Eve must have been. "Imagination," as Keats once remarked, "is my monastery and I am its monk." Our imagination can be larger than life and through it we can come into ethereal contract with distant realms and envision extraordinary possibilities. Eve lit the world ablaze and set Adam's heart on fire. God's creation was not complete until a woman stepped into the sunlight.

Unseen hands bless the morning,
Awaken nature's palette,
And restore to life a spectacle
Of vibrant colors --
Sweetening the enchanted atmosphere,
And charging it with lavish expectation:

A proper stage is set
To welcome your arrival,
Complement to nature's glory,
Adding what mere nature can't provide:
A tenderness that's templed in a smile,
A loveliness that makes the day worthwhile.

High School Reunion

hat does one say to his fellow graduates at a 55th High School reunion? 75 of the graduates, according to the information brochure, have already passed on to another world. Time engraves memories on the heart, but it also keeps its appointments with the grave. Yet something continues in a living form. Re-union means to unite again. It is a noble retort against the sweep of time. If nothing else, a reunion affirms the value of fraternal loyalty.

For Carl Sandburg, "Poetry is an echo asking a shadow to dance." The days when we were nourished by our Alma Mater are gone, yet we can still "Wake up the echoes cheering her name." Time passes, but loyalty, piety, and friendship endure. These virtues transcend whatever meaning remains for a dancing shadow.

54

Time, the great engraver,
Has left its mark,
More on some than others;

Yet our hearts still beat
With noontide passion;

Not for children of the future,
But for friends of yesterday,
With sweet solicitude and
wisdom
Purified of foolish ways;

Hands and hugs are milestones
That embrace an age,
Which chronicles a lifetime,

Holding firm what counts the
most:
Loving loyalty that will not die.

TV or not TV

reated things are darkness in so far as they proceed from nothing" (*Creatura est tenebra inquantum est ex nihilo*). These words of St. Thomas Aquinas impress upon us, with convincing force, the ontological reasonableness of being humble. We were once "nothing" and something of that character will always stay with us. If there is any hope for us, it is associated with the Light that flows from God. The light from creatures will always be an adequate replacement for the Light of God. The TV is always prominently displayed in hotel rooms, while the Bible is hidden in a drawer.

Samuel Butler's anti-utopian work, *Erewhon* is "nowhere" spelled backwards (though imperfectly). We may think we are doing well "now here," though we may still be "nowhere". A glittering Utopia carries us nowhere.

God said, "Let there be light,"
and there was light,
The world said, "Let there be glitter,"
and there was gloom;
For glitter is light
without illumination,
The inglorious attempt
to outshine the Light of God.

Light is Light only at the Source,
and every light must glow within that Flame;
It is not better to turn on the TV
than to curse the solitude;
For light that is not Light
is solitude –
Only the illuminating Light can satisfy,
the hypnotizing light enslaves.

John said, "God is Light"
that enlightens every man,
The world said, "lighten up"
and cued the enveloping darkness;
For light apart from God
is nothing less than darkness,
A lightless beacon
guiding sightless souls now here nowhere.

Social Conditioning

ccording to Aristotle, a poet must have a good eye for resemblances. T. S. Eliot said it more cryptically: "I am constantly amalgamating disparate experiences."

In our world of political correctness, strict conformity is often a requirement for job security. Being "part of the team" is one thing, but the total surrender of one's personality is quite another. The dissolution of an ice cube in a cup of hot coffee, to the poetic eye, resembles an individual trying to hang on to some measure of his personality, but finally succumbing to the impersonal requirements of his position. Social Conditioning is also a parable warning against a separation from God and an excessive conformity to the world.

The ice cube enters
a cup of steaming hot coffee
and is immediately engulfed
in a merciless environment;

No match for its enveloping foe,
it bobs and twists in futile protest
as it quickly and inexorably loses size and shape
until but a smattering of self remains –
a speck on the horizon of extinction;

And then, in a blink,
it drowns and disappears –
lost through liquefaction,
and Lethe's hypnotic powers;

Defeated, dissolved,
dispersed into its environment,
it is now thoroughly conditioned,
politically correct,
and qualified for promotion.

PLANE TALK

hat is the genesis of a poem? How is it nurtured into an expression? The English poet, William Wordsworth, may have said it best when he commented that "Poetry is the spontaneous overflow of powerful feelings: it takes its origin from emotion recollected in tranquility."

The dull sound of the airplane motor puts me in a tranquil mood in which an inner thought, attached to some emotional experience, rises like a dream and becomes the sole occupant of my attention. In such a manner, that important someone appears, and, like an angel, blesses my near sleep. The airplane contains me just as I contain the image of that special other person.

My arms are metal wings;
My tail is pointed west;
My nose bends toward Detroit
Where I'll finally come to rest;

My altitude's thirty thousand feet;
My speed, five hundred miles
For every hour I travel.
According to my dials;

My body sleeps a weary band,
A traveling troop that seems
To find its cares dissolving
In a wonder-world of dreams;

In seat nought-eight-dash D
For a mind that's nearly spent,
My engine stirs a Queen to life
With a smile that's heaven-sent.

THE SHOUT HEARD 'ROUND THE NATION

he Boston Red Sox had gone 86 years without winning a World Series Championship. The near-misses, bizarre occurrences, and countless strokes of ill-luck moved Boston Globe journalist Dave Shaughnessy to pen *The Curse of the Bambino*. The legend grew that the Sox were cursed because they had foolishly and unforgivably sold Babe Ruth to their bitter rivals, the New York Yankees. Hell would freeze before the Red Sox would ever become champions again. Yet this motley 2004 group, "Idiots," as they called themselves, won the American League pennant and defeated the St. Louis Cardinals in four straight games to claim the World Championship of Baseball.

For members of Red Sox Nation, the victory could be compared with what Ralph Waldo Emerson retold in the most celebrated poem ever written on the American Revolution, "Concord Hymn," in which he honored "the embattled farmers" who "fired the shot heard 'round the world."

Four score and a half dozen years ago,
A span of time that teemed with woe,
A curse of desperation
Haunted Red Sox Nation;

But now the torture's over, Babe,
For the comeback that these "Idiots" made
In conquering the Yankees in their yard
And knocking down a House of Cards

Has set their fandom on a roar
And crowned them champs of 2004;
They did not wait for Hell to freeze,
Their flag now flaps to autumn's breeze.

A Chilling Tale

hildren may not be poets, though they see the world poetically. It will be some time before they can pen a proper phrase. Heaven lies about us in our infancy," said William Wordsworth. As we age, however, we often lose the sense that everything is "appareled in celestial light". Perhaps this is why André Marois remarked that, "To become a poet is to remain a child" and Charles Pierre Baudelaire added that, "Genius is the rediscovery of childhood."

Let us travel back to childhood and imagine that our snow-capped back yard is planet Pluto and that we are intrepid astronauts embarking on a dangerous mission. We have nothing to fear because mom, at mission control, will bring us back safely to reality.

Two intrepid astronauts
Explore the white terrain
--Stark, immense, unbroken, terrifying--
Of backyard planet Pluto,
Wobbling in bloated space suits
Packed in wool, cotton, and mother's love;
Undaunted, plunging onward
Until their harrowing mission is complete.

Safely back at space command,
--Weary, wary, wiser, cold--
Through tears and shakes and shivers,
Their chilling tale is told;
Yet they win no praise or glory
Despite their bold encounter
With frost and wind and snow,

But their mother's stern reminder,
"Didn't I tell you so?"

A Brief Farewell

ow does one keep memories alive? A gift is appropriate, but when a gift is not in order, a poem will serve the purpose. A poem may seem to be an ineffective protector for a fading reminiscence, but that is a misjudgment of the world. Edmund Burke, not known as a poet, indicated that he knew something about poetry when he referred to it as "the art of substantiating shadows."

If a memory is a shadow, it can materialize in the imagination through the power of the right concatenation of words. Robert Frost tells us that, "Poetry is a way of remembering that which it would impoverish us to forget." I would add, "A beautiful way". We become spiritual poor when we lose hold of precious experiences that are dispatched to oblivion.

Should I write a poem
Before I head for home,
Impressing heart-prints on a page
For your quiet moments to engage
The memory of a fleeting comet
That cannot leave without a sonnet?

Paying tribute by the word
Since its voice cannot be heard;
Syllables of thanks in metered praise
Offered so that passing days
Do not dissolve in the mist of time
But are infused by this simple rhyme?

If it brings your soul some good,
Then, by heaven, I think I should.

CHANGE OF RESIDENCE

owels breathe life into words. It may very well be that so many great operas were written in Italian because that language has a perfect alternation between vowels and consonants. Polish words, on the other hand, are not well structured for operatic expression. Abbreviations, such as those that appear in telephone directories, can squeeze out the vowels. The concern in this instance is not to retain the music of a name, but to reduce space in order to save money.

My friend, whose life was once like an abbreviation, confessed to me her past mistakes, a delicate matter that the reader will understand when reading the words, "life once hushed in you". The reader will also be able to reconstruct her new place of residence by inserting e, a, u, and e in their proper places to bring Stkt back to life. The good news is that she has now launched a very successful pro-life mission that provides important help for needy women.

Setauket, NY 11733

The Yellow Pages told me
That you came from Stkt,
A curious place bereft of vowels,
Devoid of breath to resonate between four stony
consonants
And give them life;
Alien and airless,
Impoverished and prayerless.

And then I met your unabbreviated self,
Heard the music of the e a u and e
That told me a song was singing in you once again,
A melody strong enough to carry you beyond
That vowel-less residence of yesterday
And sweet enough to bring to other souls
The life that once was hushed in you
And now is shared fourfold
And who knows how much more.

WORDS

psychologist at Penn State University has reported that words conveying care or thoughtfulness can reduce the increase of proteins, such as Interleukin-6 and tumor necrosis factor-alpha, which impair the immune system. Stated more simply, words can heal. King David knew this without the benefit of science when, in Psalm 107:20, he wrote: "He sent out his word and healed them". For Isaiah (40:8), "The grass withers, the flower fades, but the word of God will stand forever." In Proverbs 12:18 we read, "Reckless words pierce like a sword, but the tongue of the wise brings healing."

God's Word is eternal. The Bible, a collection of words, is "a never-fading fund from which you draw but do not drain". The Christian poet subordinates all his words for the Word. By participating in the Word, words gain the power to heal.

I bring you
a bouquet
of words;
scentless and colorless,
bodiless and bloodless,
ethereal emissaries that rise
from realms of love
too subtle for
embodiment in the flesh;
harbingers from the heart.
delivering their unwithering message
to precincts of your inner self,
attired in lettered lightness,
nothing more;

Resistant to decline,
they are, indeed, a lasting citadel
that stand against
the tyranny of time,
outlasting fate,
surviving cosmic death;
a never-fading fund from which
you draw but do not drain;

Wrap my armless missal round your soul;
give its healing touch
the power to make you whole.

THE
COLD WAR

e are mortal organisms. Although we aspire to higher things, we are subject to being invaded by micro-organisms. This could be regarded as humiliating. Creatures made in the image of God should not be set low by organisms that are devoid of consciousness, care, or conscience. Yet, the right kind of humility can go a long way, especially when it is combined with patience. The cold war sets the stage for more important encounters. It is a respite to strengthen the immune system and prepare us for bigger battles. We will serve goodness, truth, and justice on that battlefield where we meet evil, mendacity, and injustice. The victory over a cold is simply a dress rehearsal for our victory over sin.

You have a cold,
So I am told,
Nature against nature
Locked in a grim civil war;
Loveless micro-organisms
Unaware of the citadel
Against which they strike,
Blindly, selfishly, seeking their own end,
Not caring what distress they bring
To their gracious and innocent host.

Patience and Time are your twin allies
Whose powers will prove decisive,
Yet presage larger clashes and more important
victories.
This cold war is but a rehearsal,
A way of preparation;
The tandem of your patience and God's Time
Will serve you well in battles yet to come;

Rest and rise, dear, stronger and more wise;
This skirmish won, seek now a greater prize.

ON OUR
45TH
ANNIVERSARY

he poet is an economist par excellence. He uses a single word to represent heaven and earth, a single image to embrace the family and the galaxy. But his frugality is not stingy. Rather, it opens a cornucopia of riches.

Reflecting on our marriage, which has given birth to five children and 12 grandchildren, on our November 18th wedding anniversary, it seemed to me that our extended family and God's benevolence were always intertwined. God's love is like the light from a lighthouse. Its beams appear and re-appear. During the interlunations, it seemed that we did most of the work. But in retrospect, God was always there just as the lighthouse remains even when it is not casting its guiding light.

Two score and five circlings of the sun
And has the life we started just begun?

Around our own solar center spins
Five planets and a dozen stars;
What offspring will they produce in time
To further populate the galaxy
Consisting of what earthlings call a family?

A small beginning, it was verified,
On a document now faded by the passing years
But wedded to creative love, it grew and multiplied—
The light of God's benevolence appears and re-
appears.

THE SCRAPBOOK

oets are fond of exploiting double-meaning words. Consider Hilaire Belloc's celebrated phrase: "His sins were scarlet, but his books were read." Dante often used words that had triple meanings.

The newlyweds were scrapbook hobbyists. A "scrap" is a small part that is left over. Or it is a quarrel. The gift of a special scrapbook was in order, one that would not be a chronicle of their disputations, but a record of images and events that would rejuvenate the history of their life together. All the scraps taken together reproduce a meal. It is entropy in reverse. To remember is to re-member, which is to reattach something so that that whole is not lost.

May all your "scraps" be the gentle kind:
Life's unfolding remnants that you'll find

Kept alive upon these pages,
A parable in progressive stages;

Leaves of a bright New Testament
Fluttering a message permanent,

Revealing through remembered parts,
The rhythm of two loving hearts.

The Peaceable Kingdom

dward Hicks (1780-1849), during his lifetime, was better known as a Quaker preacher. Posterity knows him as the gifted painter of 61 versions of "The Peaceable Kingdom," a theme inspired by a passage in Isaiah 11:6-8 where it is written that "the wolf will live with the lamb, the leopard will lie down with the goat, the calf and the lion and yearling together."

My two-year-old grandchild used my face as the terrain to create her own peaceable kingdom. Her assemblage of animals would be tame and friendly. What better lesson could I teach her than encouraging her to share in the orchestration of a future world where peace abides and gentleness is rewarded?

She surveys her grandpa's face
And finds,
Not an ageing countenance,
Nor a tender smile,
But a broad terrain for beasts to roam;
One by one, with exquisitely deft child-fingers,
She peels the paper backs from her wild menagerie
And sets each species free to dot her living, loving
landscape
Made motionless and silent by command;
On the grassy plain above his brow
She sets the noble giraffe,
A horse appears,
Stilly galloping across his former cheek;
From his erstwhile ear a monkey finds its home,
And his forehead now accommodates the jackal and
the lamb,
Who happily live in unaccustomed peace;
No cosmetologist ever studied her client
With such rapt intent:
A lion to perch upon his nose,
A rhino to accentuate his chin,
A bear to seal an eyelid,
A cat to grace his neck,
"Just one more left,"
She says with sympathetic tone,
And sticks a hippopotamus firmly on his lips;
Ferocity extinguished, beastliness annulled,
She smiles at the outcome of her big and playful
game;
"What are grandpas for," he thinks,
"But to pacify and tame."

TO ISAAC

n Hebrew, the name means "he laughs" and is loosely hidden in the fifth line of his welcoming poem. Both nature and poets love to hide. Demosthenes is known as the "laughing philosopher". Little Isaac will be serenaded long before he learns to laugh, for his mom and two sisters are accomplished songstresses. For Thomas Carlyle, poetry is "musical thought". "See deep enough," he went on to say, "and you see musically; the heart of nature being everywhere music."

"The hills are alive with the sound of music." And so is Isaac's household. In time and with proper training he will join the other singers in his family and form a quartet that will rival that of Rigoletto.

Into four loving hearts and eight eager arms,
Trying their best to keep you from all harms,
Nurturing, naturing, nourishing,
They witness you prodigious flourishing;

Looking at how innocently your eyes act,
We wonder how one so compact
With such a delicate constitution
Can start a major revolution
And turn the household upside down
Like a mischievous and clumsy clown.

Sing along with us a song of joy,
We are so pleased you are a boy,
Right now you are quite operatic,
A quality not problematic
Since your manly voice, we all agree,
Will complement our divas three.

ON TURNING
SEVENTY

ercy Bysshe Shelley spoke of poetry as "Arresting the vanishing apparitions that haunt the interlunations of life." Literally, an "interlunation" is the time between two full moons. Figuratively, it is what transpires between an event and its repetition. A table was set at a fine eating establishment and, after an interval, was re-set. But what transpired during the interval, seemingly erased by the re-setting of the table, was something worth capturing, as poem's capture fugitive messages that are headed toward oblivion.

Poetry prevents the passage of time from bringing things to naught. A matriarch, presiding over five children and a dozen grandchildren should be stored in the annals of the heart as well as on the pages of eternity.

The long table was set for twenty-two
and draped in white;
The coffee carafes and the orange juice
glasses were filled,
While purpose and expectation
filled the room.

A matriarch had turned three-score and ten,
An occasion for feast and celebration,
But more importantly, a time to honor one
Whose love had touched the hearts
of all the members present.

When the room finally emptied
at the appointed hour,
Servants entered to restore it
to its former pristine state,
But they could not erase what had transpired;

The salute from twenty-one found its way
to that region of the heart
Where it will continue to reside,
impervious to the obliterations of time
And serve as an ever accessible reminder of
A harvest day when the rewards
of love came home.

LAURA

he was the maid of honor at a wedding. Her name was Laura, one that evokes its multiple meanings in Italian. It is the name of Petrarch's love to whom he wrote the beautiful sonnets that she, because of her illiteracy, could never read. Yet, for the celibate poet, she was alone for him, woman *("Che sola a me par donna.")*.

My friend yearned to be the only one for someone. Her soul was artistic and she loved to paint. But, contrary to her sensibilities, she was consigned to working as a bank teller. She had cut her finger and wrapped it in an over-sized bandage, hoping that it would provoke a conversation with a special someone. I wrote her poem, passed it through her teller's window and never saw her again. Poetry can establish a sympathetic compact, but its potentialities are severely limited.

I could not tell the world
my heart was sore,

And yet I could not bear
my state alone;

I wisely re-assigned
the torment at my core

To an injured finger pleading in
a language of its own;

For neither clerks nor clients
do believe

That one should wear a tortured heart
upon a raveled sleeve.

I found an exotic bandage
with an outlandish tale to tell

Of terrifying dinosaurs
with vengeance in their eyes

And spikes and bear-trap teeth
and a wicked place to dwell -

My own neglected heart, no doubt,
in pre-historical disguise.

Cash and checks and studied smiles
passed in endless streams,

But no one ever spoke to me
of dinosaurs or dreams.

One day he will arrive, I know,
And in my presence linger;

And he will read my heart all right,
without need of scripted finger.

THE CHASE

hildren have a natural affection for animals. They understand instinctively how happiness can be a warm puppy. Walt Disney's recognition of this simple fact has made billions of dollars for his industry. This affinity that children have for animals may be explained in part because they are all creatures that emanate from the Hand of God. It may be highly unnatural, then, for children to be atheists. A toy may be enjoyable or even educational, but a cat, a dog, or a rabbit, is a mate, and an intimation of the Creator.

Saint Francis of Assisi, who retained the heart of a child, addressed various animals as his "brothers" and his "sisters". When he preached to the birds, it is easy for us to imagine that they listened to him.

Two tiny tots, two and three,
Who shared the same birth date and
An unbridled enthusiasm for opening presents,
Tore into their gifts, impatiently
Trying to extricate the hidden treasures
(made in China or in some other exotic place)
that were mummified within miles of
multi-colored wrapping paper
Until,
Their actions were interrupted and voices rendered
mute
By the unexpected appearance of Brother Rabbit;
The children dashed to the patio railing,
Beheld an authentic *Lepus americanus*
(made in heaven, like themselves)
And peered at their furry visitor—
Who stood transfixed with twitching nose,
Twenty feet away in distance,
Eons in evolutionary time—
Childhood awe meeting rabbit fear,
A brief, hypnotic, kindred encounter;
Then, in a vain attempt to apprehend him,
They sent Señor Rabbit, moving with the speed of
fright,
Bounding from the yard, but not from his pursuers'
hearts.

The Prism

prism, at least the kind that Sir Isaac Newton used, is a transparent object that separates white light into a spectrum of colors. It is a device used that allows something to reveal its inner secrets. A child's tear is a prism that refracts and foretells the episodes of her future life. The heart understands prisms in a way that no scientist ever can. The tear of a one-year-old child anticipates the crises of her lifetime, just as the DNA in the one-celled zygote foretells the completion of one's anatomy. There will be frustrations, disappointments, hurts, and complications. They are needed to forge a soul. This momentary tear will quickly fade away, but will be followed by others that are needed to form one's character. Hans Christian Anderson's mermaid had no tears. But because of this privation, "she suffers so much more."

A lingering tear,
the final remnant of her now forgotten hurt,
beclouds a wide and searching eye;
a watery prism refracting
across my heart
a rainbow Sir Isaac Newton never saw --
a spectrum of emotions flashing forth
a span of life, yet squeezed into a single drop
of vibrant liquid whose quivering tale
is far more touching
than words could ever be:
a fleeting sorrow, prelude to
its stronger kin;
hope undashed, faith unsoiled,
and love as yet untarnished,
fledglings to be tested and re-formed;
innocence and bravery,
youth's pure sweetness, childhood's trust --
primordial elements
that Love and Time
conspire through labyrinthine twists and turns
to form and frame a soul.

A "Fish" With a Future

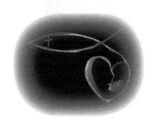

ur third child and his wife came over to our house with a tape, one that replayed a few seconds of the play that was unfolding within the pregnant mom. Our first grandchild looked like a fish as she delicately maneuvered within the amniotic sac. It would not be long before our marine virtuoso was looking at the same screen where she made her TV debut, but this time sitting on her grandpa's lap and watching a fish named Cleo and a frightful whale named Monstro. The tape belongs to time frozen. Our grandchild evolves in time unbound. Origins can be deceiving. They can conceal he germ of realities that require decades to reveal. In the words of G. K. Chesterton, "If seeds in the black earth can turn into such beautiful roses, what might not the heart of man become in its long journey toward the stars?

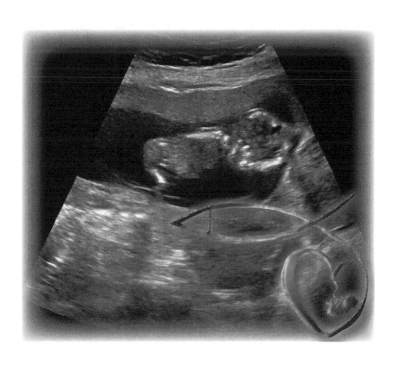

Excitedly, they pushed the tape –
Product of Ultra-Sound –
Into the machine,
And we watched in awe
As a "fish" filled the screen
And shimmied before our eyes.

Which was more magical?
The electronic image remains the same,
But its living counterpart has metamorphosed,
Becoming, herself, an enchanted spectator,
Curling her delicate fingers around
Her Grandpa's neck

In awe of Monstro the Whale
Who fills the very same screen
Where she made her watery debut,
Oblivious to the love and joy
She would bring
That would swim into our hearts.

Should Old Aquinas Be Forgot?

he secular world is so preoccupied with being up-to-date that it forgets, as C. S. Lewis reminds us, that "All that is not eternal is eternally out of date." To suggest that the thought of St. Thomas Aquinas is "quaint" and not relevant to our modern age is a curiosity. The man who labors to be in step with his times dooms himself to be out of step with the times that follow. Why do people sacrifice themselves on the altar of irrelevancy? Aquinas endures because of his common sense, and because he sought the truth of things. These two traits are evident in his Commentary on Matthew where he states that "Life comes before learning: for life leads to the knowledge of truth." His wisdom is timeless. "The immutability of what wisdom has acquired," writes Jacques Maritain, in praising the Angelic Doctor, "is not in time, but above it, and far from stopping history, accelerates its course and the progress of knowledge."

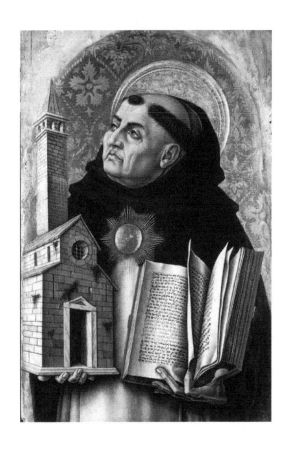

"Quaint" was the word they used!
How quaint a way itself
To dub the man whose influence
Endures in forms diverse and ever new:
In song and stone, in text and verse,
In papal declaration;
In minds and hearts, in life and law,
And festive celebration.

How could a misplaced adjective
Entomb in time what Time could not?
The bellow of this ox still sounds,
Nor can he be forgot;
He soars beyond all fashions, frenzies,
Fancies, fads, political musts;
He has outlived all vogues and trends -
Those flashing ephemera now turned to dust.

The passing years but magnify
The glory of this saint;
And those acquainted with his spirit
Are one in stressing, "Quaint' he ain't".

poet, I suppose, would notice the metaphysical significance of flickering lights on a Christmas tree. The lights flicker between light and darkness. It is a metaphor for us often half-hearted creatures who fluctuate between grace and gravity. "Purity of heart," wrote Kierkegaard is "to will one thing". The adjustment, the turning to God, is within easy reach. But how reluctant we often are to make that simple adjustment and serve God unreservedly.

Politics is an area where compromise can be prudent. The Christmas tree, however, points in one direction – upward. Christianity demands unbroken fidelity and uncompromised allegiance. Christ is a power plant dispensing grace; we are energized by virtue of our firm connection with Him. A loose connection, by flirting with darkness, cannot be faithful to the light.

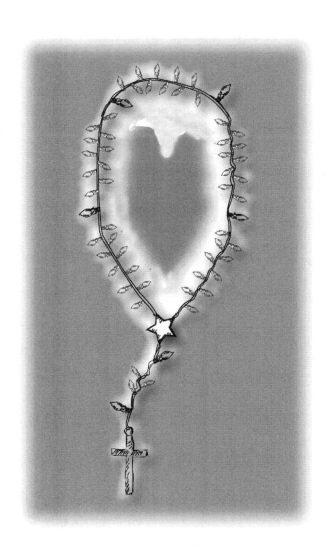

Fluttering, flittering, flickering,
They oscillate between darkness and light,
Indecisive, inconstant, and irresolute,
They flash their tale of ambiguity;

But simple twists of the fingers,
Clockwise turns to the right,
Return the lights to their source,
Uniting the many to One;

No longer flirting with darkness,
They glow with a steady glow,
Reliable beacons reminding us
How close we once were to the darkness,
How near we are now to the Light.

Victim of McProgress

he worst enemy of life, freedom and the common decencies," wrote Aldous Huxley, "is total anarchy; their second worst enemy is total efficiency." The author of Brave New World, we should note, speaks with authority. Efficiency can be an enemy to loyalty, creativity, and personality. The greatest reward for the server at a fast food restaurant is not serving food, but offering and receiving friendship. Efficiency may improve the profits, but it can erode the *joie de vivre* of the workplace.

If progress is their most important product, as certain corporations claim, then employees become their most undeserving victims. Alienation increases as our society becomes more streamlined. Chatter is time wasted; greetings must be perfunctory; serving coffee becomes serving time.

No, I was not downsized,
My workplace was upsized,
And I am downhearted;

****

I used to serve friends,
But now I serve coffee
In our new, expanded, state-of-the-art
Environment that knows nothing
Of my ache-in-the-heart.

****

We are now more modern, efficient, streamlined,
and sanitized,
But friends who once sweetened my morning with
a smile
And warmed my spirits with kind words
No longer linger within view,
Having disappeared behind obstructing walls,
Privatized, compartmentalized, ostracized;

****

Who will bring me Splenda for my sorrow,
Or a cup of kindness to colorize my mood
So that I can be prepared to greet tomorrow
When I will serve my patrons more than food?

A Basket of Food

here is food for the body, food for thought, and food for the soul. My friend is on an exceedingly strict diet that permits her to eat and digest very few items that are listed on earth's multifarious menu. Fortunately, she welcomes feasts of a spiritual kind which means that she is not allergic to the Holy Spirit.

Through ordinary digestion, food is transformed into us. By a process of assimilation, food becomes part of our physical being. But when our spirit partakes of beauty, truth, and goodness, we are uplifted by them. C. S. Lewis, in his poem, *On a Theme From Nicolas of Cusa*, points out that when we digest "their ray," we become "luminous as they". Thus, as St. Thomas Aquinas maintains, it is better to know God than to devour a meal.

I present you with a basket of food,
But alert to all your allergies,
Have omitted all legumes and in their place,
Please find my heartfelt admiration for your
gentleness and your grace.

You'll find no violent fruits in here,
For I have substituted grateful thanks
In honor of the courage you display
And the humor you exhibit that gets you through
the day.

I also have withheld starches of all kinds,
In lieu of abundant blessings for your soul;
And for those angry liquids that cause you
consternation
I offer you my prayers and joyful salutations.

No candy nor desserts are here contained,
But in their stead, a pledge of faithful friendship.
I have diligently left out all items that are
questionable,
And trust you'll find this spiritual bouquet,
perfectly digestible.

Christmas

hristmas is about birth and rebirth. It is about the birth of our Savior and our own rebirth. It is the great antidote to life that is hurdling toward death. Poetry is also about birth and rebirth. In its own humble way, it, too, is an argument against death being the final chapter of our lives. Virgil, the greatest of the Latin poets, said that "There are tears in things, and all things that are doomed to die touch the heart" (*Lachrimae rerum; et mentem mortalia tangunt*). But he did not know about Christmas and how the birth of the Christ-child means the victory of light over darkness, love over hate, and life over death. Christmas brings back to life so many fond memories of friends we have almost forgotten. Mortality continues to elicit tears, but Christmas, that transcends our finitude, is the great harbinger of unfettered joy and lasting life.

The birth of Christ stirs our memories that may
have been
Dormant, like a child's slumber, for nearly a dozen
months,
Occasioning a second birth to a myriad of friends
our hearts hold dear,
Evoking pleasant times, bright smiles, warm hugs,
and joy-filled conversations.

Our memories, like swaddling clothes, wrap you
with our affection as we await,
Like shepherds in the field, the birth of a Sceptered
Babe
Who rules without power and loves without
restraint:
Our light, our hope, our path to lasting peace.

To all, on this Eve of Christmas,
Our love, our thanks and our sincerest wish
That you remember our gift of friendship
So we can share it for another year.

Evergreen

he distinguished poet and literary critic, John Crowe Ransom, has stated that "The poet perpetuates in his poem an order of existence which in actual life is constantly crumbling beneath is touch." My Christmas writing paper displays a smiling snowman surrounded by an extensive snowscape dotted with numerous evergreen trees. The contrast between the snowman and the trees is striking and brings to mind the theological notion that our mortality is linked to our immortality through hope. Even the prosaic can remind us of the association between our fragile nature and our eternal destiny. When children playfully build a snowman, they are lost in the moment, absorbed by the fun of it all. The poet, however, sees an order of existence that has eternal significance. His words give witness to that higher order so that we are less likely to be contained by the immanent.

THE FIR'S
SNOWEL

Despite his smile and cheerful disposition,
Our snow man's life is but an intermission
Between two periods of warmer weather –
This cold snap will not last forever.

****

Ephemeral creation of winter's rage,
He celebrates what cannot age:
Those aspiring trees that dot the scene
Which, like our hope, stay ever green

Other Books by Dr. Donald DeMarco:

How to Remain Sane in a World That Is Going Mad

Abortion in Perspective

Sex and the Illusion of Freedom

Today's Family in Crisis

The Anesthetic Society

The Shape of Love

The Incarnation in a Divided World

In My Mother's Womb

Hope for a World without Hope

Chambers of the Heart

How to Survive as a Catholic in a Parochial World

Character in a Time of Crisis

The Many Faces of Virtue

Timely Thoughts for Timeless Catholics

New Perspectives in Contraception

The Integral Person in a Fragmented World

Patches of God-Light

The Heart of Virtue

Virtue's Alphabet from Amiability to Zeal

Biotechnology and the Assault on Parenthood

Architects of the Culture of Death

Being Virtuous in a non-Virtuous World

The Value of Life in a Culture of Death

A Family Portfolio in Poetry and Prose

How to Flourish in a Fallen World